W9-BDP-157

Left-handed knitting

REGINA HURLBURT

DRAWINGS BY PRUE CAMPBELL-SMITH

VNR VAN NOSTRAND REINHOLD COMPANY
New York   Cincinnati   Toronto   London   Melbourne

Copyright © 1977 by Litton Educational Publishing, Inc.
Library of Congress Catalog Card Number 77-77972
ISBN 0-442-23585-2

Printed in the United States of America

Published in 1977 by Van Nostrand Reinhold Company
A division of Litton Educational Publishing, Inc.
450 West 33rd Street, New York, NY 10001, U.S.A.

Van Nostrand Reinhold Limited
1410 Birchmount Road, Scarborough, Ontario M1P 2E7, Canada

Van Nostrand Reinhold Australia Pty. Limited
17 Queen Street, Mitcham, Victoria 3132, Australia

Van Nostrand Reinhold Company Limited
Molly Millars Lane, Wokingham, Berkshire, England

16 15 14 13 12 11 10 9 8 7 6 5 4 3 2 1

Library of Congress Cataloging in Publication Data

Hurlburt, Regina.
  Left-handed knitting.

   1. Knitting. I. Title.
TT820.H87   746.4'32   77-77972
ISBN 0-442-23585-2

Left-handed knitting

This book is the natural progression of my learning processes. Having learned to needlepoint, as I wrote in LEFT-HANDED NEEDLEPOINT, it seemed most natural to return to an even more basic handcraft, knitting. Perhaps the subtle influence of our times, the condition of the world today, leads us to search for the basics.

Again, I hope that this simple book will help teach others, give them pleasure and pride in their own self-made garments, and for the left-handed needlecrafter, give a little easing of tensions and frustrations.

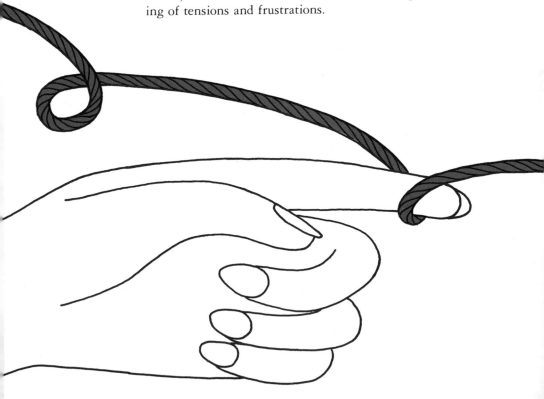

Contents

A Bit of History

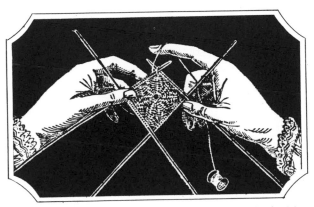

The Royal Victoria Knitting Book, published 1851.
Courtesy of the Victoria & Albert Museum, London.

Knitting is the handcraft of creating a textile by the manipulation of a single thread.

The origin of knitting is said to have been in Coptic Egypt. A fragment of knitted fabric found in the excavations of ancient Fostat, the original settlement of Cairo, showed a fine Arab fabric woven with two needles and a single strand of yarn.

Knitting as we know it today may have originated with the Arabs and spread through the Mediterranean countries, then to Spain with the Moors, and to France with Arabic traders and sailors.

The shipwrecked sailors of the Spanish Armada are credited with bringing knitting and knitting patterns to Scotland and Ireland. Some of the traditional Scottish patterns bear a great similarity to ancient Arabic designs that were brought to Spain by the Moors.

The wool-producing countries of northern Europe developed wool knitting as their skilled craft, whereas silk knitting developed in Italy as a result of the Venetian trade with China. We can thank the Italians for the introduction of silk knitted hose, a privilege for the wealthy at the time.

Knitting in the medieval era was mainly a matter for men since it was considered a business or a trade and strictly controlled by guilds. At home needlework was for the entire family and not considered of much importance, although it kept the families clothed and warm.

The Industrial Revolution and the invention of knitting machinery brought about a lowering of standards of the knitted goods and fabrics. This in turn helped to bring forth the higher quality of handcrafted wearing apparel, further helped by the improvement of the quality of the wools and silks in both textures and dyes.

In the middle of the eighteenth century the change in fashion and social structure brought about another change in knitting— the use of cotton yarns. Silk had always been too costly for the many, wool too coarse for the elegant. With the rising cotton trade, a middle-class society turned to cotton for their knitting yarns.

Through the centuries that have followed, handcrafts in all three fibers have continued to grow. Nowadays the yarns used by the hand knitter are no longer a symbol of his or her place in the social structure.

Today knitting is used for both decoration and warmth. The introduction of synthetics and yarns of varied thickness and type has given us enormous advantage over our ancestors.

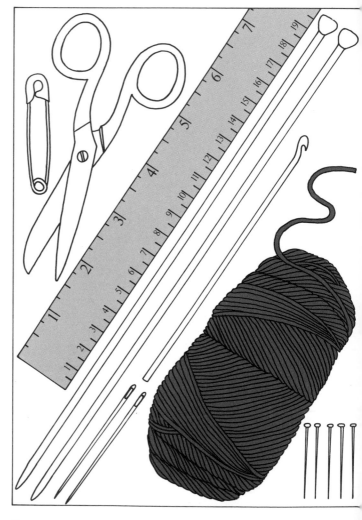

Needles and Yarns

The following pages will give you the basic information that you should have regardless of which hand you use in your knitting. It is essential to know about your tools, yarns and tension, the abbreviations used in knitting instructions, and other tips to make your work enjoyable.

Needles

Knitting needles are manufactured in various lengths of metal, wood, or plastic. Generally smaller-gauge needles are metal; larger gauge, wood or plastic. I do recommend that you take good care of your needles. They should be kept flat in a needle-holder and always clean from hand dirt, as this can be transferred to your yarn as you are working. Don't allow your wood or plastic needles to become nicked or warped: this can damage your yarn or affect its tension. Needles are usually sold in pairs. The most common ones are pointed at one end, with a knob or stop at the other. These are used for flat knitting, and the rows are worked forth and back.

For working in the round, there are two kinds of needles: sets of four needles with points at both ends for small items, and the larger or longer circular needle also pointed at both ends. The obvious advantage of a circular needle is that it will give you better control if you are working with a great number of stitches. You need have no fear of stitches falling off the end of your needle. I recommend a circular needle for heavy yarns coupled with a great number of stitches, even if you are working flat (sweater, front and back) rather than round (skirt).

Whichever kind of needle you use, it is generally most comfortable to work with a slightly longer needle than required. This gives you the assurance that you will have room for all your stitches and you will not have to worry that some will slip off the needle, in which case you will have to face the task of picking up these dropped stitches. It is most important to consider your own comfort and ease. That is what will make your work enjoyable.

Always use the needle size recommended for the yarn in your pattern. The exception to this is if the tension of your knitting is not according to the prescribed instructions. I will speak more of tension later in the book.

Since so much of the world is moving to the uniformity of

Knitting Needle Sizes

American	Metric
0	2.00
1	2.50
2	2.75
3	3.25
4	3.50
5	4.00
6	4.50
7	5.00
8	5.50
9	6.00
10	6.50
10½	7.00
11	8.00
13	9.00

---

metrication, you will find the list below divided into what I shall call American and Metric. Craft shops carry such international varieties of supplies that it is best to be at home with both sizes of needles. A simple rule of thumb regarding needle sizes is: the higher the number, the thicker the needle.

The metric sizes of needles being not quite exact in relation to inch size, you will find slight variations in needle charts. Don't despair if the needle recommended is in slight variance with chart size. Always work with the size recommended in the pattern.

Yarns

Unless you are a very accomplished knitter, always purchase the yarn recommended in your pattern. It has been designed with a specific yarn in mind. The yarn should knit up to the required number of stitches to the inch. All of this is geared to give you the exact shape and size that you are working towards.

It is wise to purchase all your yarn at the same time. Dye lots vary. It may not be evident in the shop, but can be very apparent when your garment is completed. Sometimes it is wise to purchase an extra ball of yarn for testing tension or any other needs that may arise. Always check the color-code number and dye-lot number on all the balls before you leave the shop.

Wool is the traditional yarn for knitting. It is spun in various plies: two, three, and four, double knit, chunky, Aran or Aran type. It is pliant, easy to work with, and easy to press into shape. Many of today's wools may be washed without fear of shrinkage if the washing instructions are carefully followed. Some spinning mills add a small percentage of nylon or Orlon to give the wool greater strength. The only drawback of pure wool is that the drying time is longer than synthetic fibers.

Keep in mind that the thickness of plies differs from spinning mill to spinning mill. What is four-ply under one brand name may be slightly thicker or thinner than another brand. This will affect your tension and the number of stitches to the inch or centimeter.

Man-made or synthetic yarns are manufactured of minerals and chemicals. They can almost feel like and give the warmth of wool. They have the advantage of being quick-drying. It is important to knit this yarn evenly, as uneven work is not easily corrected by the pressing and blocking process.

Novelty yarns such as linen, cotton, silk, mohair, and bouclé wool are also used for knitting. These are usually not advised for beginners as they require a proficiency in controlling the tension and yarn as it slips over your finger. For the experienced worker, the mixing of two threads such as a fine wool and silk can make for an attractive texture. (A word of caution—do not team bouclé wool with a man-made fiber. They require different ways of handling tension.)

Some yarns are measured in ounces, some in grams. Your pattern may have either or, hopefully, both. If not, the table below may be of some assistance to you.

Grams	Kilograms
1 oz = 28.35 g	25 g = ⅞ oz
4 oz = 113.4 g	50 g = 1¾ oz
8 oz = 226.8 g	1 kg/1000 g = 2 lbs 2 oz
1 lb = 454 g	

When you have purchased your pattern, yarn, and needles, there are a few additional items that I recommend as useful.

The first is a receptacle to hold all your equipment. It can be either a knitting bag or just a box large enough to hold everything easily. The following are also necessities. As you become more involved and proficient in knitting you may wish to add to your equipment:

A small notebook and pencil. I heartily recommend this to keep notes regarding the rows knitted or any other record you may desire to keep of your work. If a pattern requires twelve rows of a stitch, it is so much easier to have made a record of each row as you complete it. (Never put your work down with an incomplete row, it is too easy to drop a stitch.) If you have to stop before the section is completed, you will have an exact record of completed work. It will save you the time of having to recount the rows.

A stiff twelve-inch (30.5 cm) ruler, for measuring your work. You should also use this to measure the number of stitches to the inch or centimeter in your practice square.

A strong plastic tape measure to measure yourself.

A package of blunt-tipped wool or tapestry needles for stitching the knitted sections together.

Stainless steel pins (any other kind might leave rust stains when blocking or pressing).

Stitch holders. I find that large safety pins of the blanket or diaper variety are perfectly adequate.

Crochet hooks. Convenient to pick up dropped stitches as well as another method of putting your knitted sections together.

Cable needles. These are available two or three to a package. They are marked to cover a variety of needle sizes.

A small sharp-pointed pair of scissors.

A plastic bag or towel to wrap your work. There is nothing more dispiriting than a grimy piece of unfinished work. It usually never gets finished. What a waste!

Symbols and Abbreviations

Study your pattern carefully. It is so much easier to have the various instructions clear in your mind before you begin knitting. You will then be able to work confidently.

All patterns use a series of abbreviations that are fairly standard. If you find some variations, study them carefully. If your pattern includes a stitch that you have never worked before, knit the usual four-inch (10 cm) square for fuller understanding. You might well need practice to convert the right-handed instructions for the new stitch to your own left-handed needs. Sometimes the designer will create a stitch that is to give you a different texture. The instructions will be carefully defined in the pattern.

In the list of abbreviations below some will be simple to grasp at the very beginning. For those that seem a bit more complicated, I will give instructions in later pages.

* An asterisk is usually shown as a repeat sign. For example: *K4, P4, repeat 6 times from *.

( ) Parentheses can denote two different things, depending on the pattern maker. They may enclose instructions to be repeated or instructions for different sizes, for example: K20 (24, 28, 32) sts.

[ ] Brackets. Some patterns may use square brackets as a marking for different sizes.

Patt	—	Pattern
K	—	Knit
P	—	Purl

14

Rep	— Repeat
G st	— Garter stitch
St st	— Stocking stitch
Inc	— Increase
Dec	— Decrease
M 1	— Make one stitch. This usually means to increase by one stitch. The pattern instructions will tell you exactly where.
In	— Inch (es)
Cm	— Centimeter (s)
Rs	— Right side
Sl st	— Slip stitch
Tog	— Together
Psso	— Pass slipped stitch over
Tbl	— Through back loop
Wrn	— Wool around needle
Won	— Wool over needle
Ws	— Wrong side
Kwise	— Knitwise
Pwise	— Purlwise
Y fwd	— Yarn forward
Y bk	— Yarn back
K Tw L, R	— Knit, twist left, right
Knit evenly	— Knit without changes for the required number of rows.

A last bit of advice—when beginning a new ball of yarn, always do so at the beginning of a row. Leave about six inches (15 cm) of the end of your yarn hanging down, loop the yarn of the new ball over the needle, again with about six inches (15 cm) hanging loosely, and just continue with your knitting. Eventually you will weave these loose ends into the edges of your finished work with a blunt-ended tapestry or wool needle.

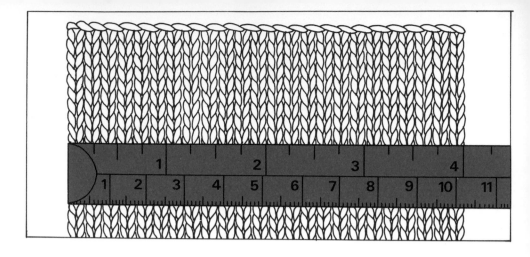

Tension

Tension simply means getting the correct number of stitches and rows of knitting to the inch or centimeter. The importance of this is stressed to give the correct size and shape to your work. All patterns will give you the tension or gauge at the beginning of the instructions. The required tension or number of stitches to the inch or centimeter is established by the designer when the design is first laid out on graph paper. The designer may well have a style of working that is completely different from your own.

There is a simple method of checking your knitting tension. Knit a sample square measuring four inches (10 cm); anything smaller will not give you enough scope to achieve a proper measure. Use the stocking stitch (knit one row, purl one row, alternately). When complete, cast off, and pin out on a flat surface. Place two pins one inch apart using your stiff ruler as a guide. Then count the number of stitches across and the number of rows down. They must agree with the pattern instructions. If your count does not—don't worry.

If you have more stitches to the inch, then you are working tighter than the designer. The way to correct that is to work another square using the next size larger needle than called for by your pattern. If you have fewer stitches, then you are working too loosely. Make another square using the next size smaller needle. Keep in mind that even a half-stitch can throw off the size of the finished piece. It is best to keep experimenting until you achieve the correct tension.

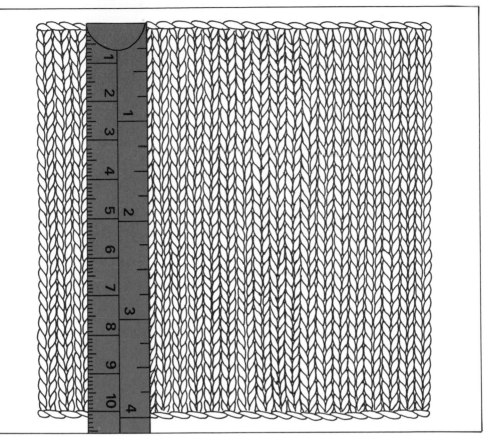

Tension measured over a four-inch square (approx 10 cm)

The stocking stitch is used as the tension gauge for all things you will knit. It is a closely knitted stitch, and if it is worked at the correct tension, then you will undoubtedly work all your various stitches correctly. All stitch tension instructions are based on the stocking stitch.

Read your pattern carefully. Underline and mark all measurements that apply to your size.

As abbreviations can differ from one pattern to another, make certain that you understand all those used in the pattern you are using. If a stitch new to you is called for, make a practice square before beginning to work.

Work carefully, knowing exactly what you are going to do before you begin to knit, and you will derive much pleasure from your work.

Two stages of making your slip knot

Casting On Stitches

There are several ways of casting on your first stitches. No matter which way you go about it, it always begins with the making of a slip knot.

The simplest and sturdiest method of casting on is with two needles. It is sometimes called the Cable Method. It will give you a firm clean edge. Some consider it perhaps to have insufficient elasticity; I prefer it for its strength. Having made your slip knot, hold that needle in your right hand, with the other needle in your left hand. Insert the tip of the left needle into the loop on the right needle from front to back. Bring your yarn around and over the tip of the left needle. Pull the loop on the left needle through the loop on the right needle. Transfer the new loop to the right needle and you will have two loops on the right needle. Insert the tip of the left needle between the two loops on the right needle and repeat the action of looping the yarn over the left needle; pull the third loop through between the two loops on the right needle and transfer it on to the right needle. Continue inserting the tip of the needle between the last two stitches on the right needle, making your loops and transferring them until you have the required number of stitches cast on to your right needle.

The second method of casting on is called the Thumb Method.

18

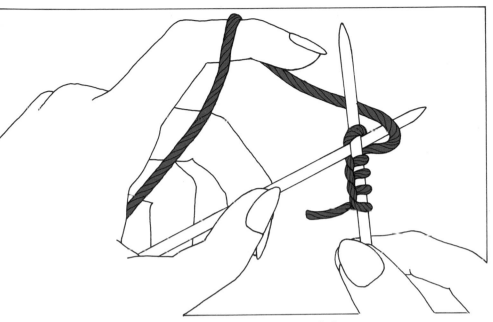

Two stages of two-needle method of casting on stitches

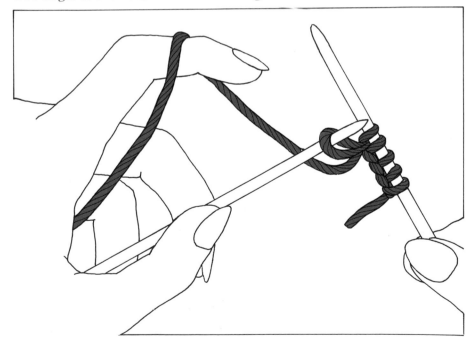

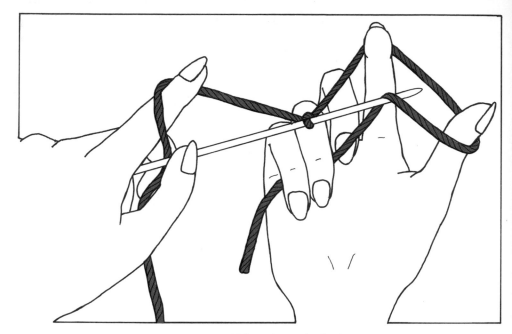

Three stages of Thumb Method of casting on

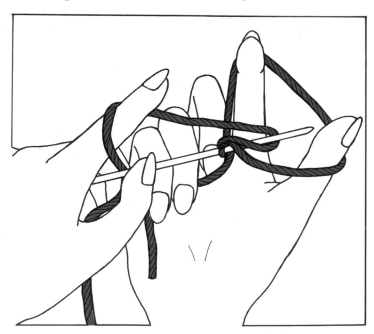

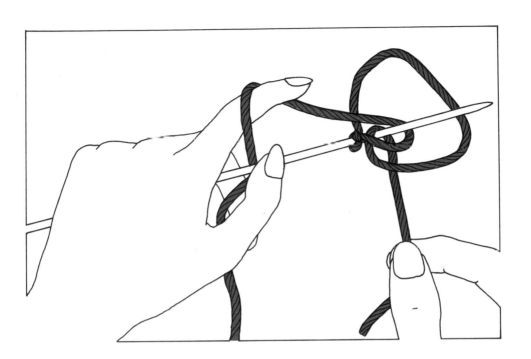

It is considered easier, faster to work and will give you a more flexible edge. It is preferred by many people.

Measure off a length of yarn sufficient to use for casting on the required number of stitches. A simple formula to follow for the length needed is a yard for every sixty stitches in medium-weight yarn. The thicker the yarn, the more should be measured off.

Make your usual first loop over a needle held in your left hand. Loop the yarn over your thumb and index finger, held slightly apart, of your right hand. Create a slight tension by using your little finger to hold the yarn in place across the palm of your hand. Hold the needle in your left hand, insert the tip under the yarn near the thumb. Loop the yarn from the ball end over and around the needle and draw through the loop over your thumb and index finger. This leaves a new stitch cast on your needle. Tighten the stitch by pulling the short end of the yarn. Loop the short end of the yarn around your thumb and index finger again and repeat the loop from the ball end of

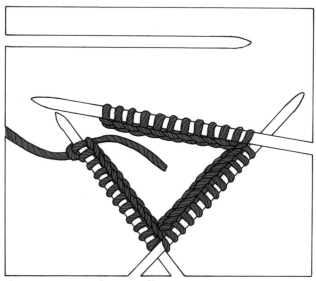

Casting on with four needles

the yarn until the required number of stitches are on your needle.

Casting on using four needles will create a round. It is used for small items such as gloves or socks that will feel much more comfortable without seams.

Use the two-needle method of casting on. You may cast on all your stitches on one needle, then divide evenly between the two other needles. Or you can divide the number of required stitches into three groups, casting one group on each of the three needles. Use a marker thread to signify the beginning of your first row. This will avoid confusion as your round grows. Use the fourth needle to begin knitting in the ordinary way. If you cast on over the three needles, be certain the yarn between the needles is not slack or twisted as the edge will not be even or smooth. Some knitters use small corks placed on the ends of the needles not being knitted at the moment to keep stitches from slipping off.

Casting on using a circular needle is a good method for working in the round to make skirts or sweaters without seams. It is useful to distribute the weight of heavy yarn so it will not be so tiring to constantly have the heavy knitting in one hand or the other. It helps to distribute stitches of heavy yarn and you need not be concerned with the dropping of a stitch. The cir-

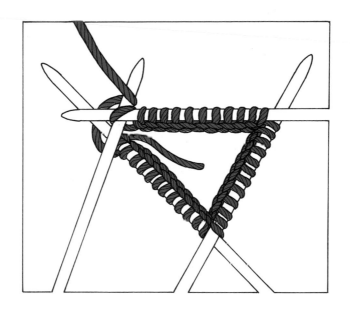

cular needle is never free of stitches as you move around and around. Therefore, after casting on and before you begin your actual knitting, place a marker thread to show where the round or row begins. It will help avoid confusion. Be certain to purchase the correct length circular needle. It must be long enough to hold all your stitches increased as you progress, in addition to the basic casting on. Your pattern will specify the length required.

Loop your yarn on your hand in any way that is comfortable for you to work. I find that once or twice around the small finger under the middle finger and perhaps once around your index finger. Never wind your yarn too tightly, just allow it to flow evenly. Too loose or too tight will affect the tension. You will achieve your own method and ease very quickly.

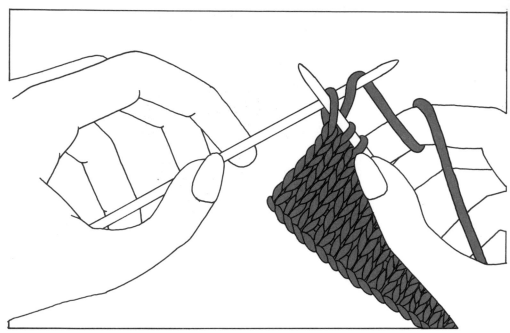

Two stages of the Knit Stitch

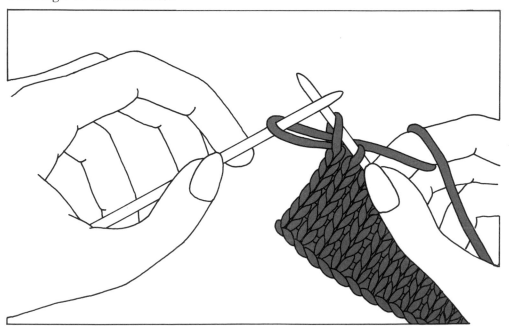

The Two Basic Stitches

The best knitting method for the left-handed is called Continental Knitting. It is a method that employs both hands. The left hand is the working hand, holding the needle that actually creates the stitches. The right hand holds the yarn and guides it. The right hand also holds the needle from which you will work the stitch on to the left needle.

Knit Stitch. Hold your yarn in back of the right needle with the cast-on stitches. Insert point of left needle into first cast-on stitch on right needle and pick up loop on to your left needle, pulling loop through to the front of your work. When the loop is safely on your left needle, then allow the stitch on your right needle to drop off. Repeat this until all the stitches on your right needle have been worked and transferred to your left needle.

Transfer the empty needle to your left hand and continue working the same stitch as much as required.

These knitted rows form a pattern called the Garter Stitch, which is a strong, closely worked texture.

Purl Stitch. Hold the needles as you did for the knit stitch; working needle in your left hand and the needle with your stitches in your right hand. The right hand will again guide and hold the yarn. For this stitch bring your yarn to the front of your needle. Insert the left needle point into the front of the stitch on the right needle so that both the ball yarn and the stitch are to the front of the left needle. Wind the yarn over and around the left needle and pull it through the stitch on the right needle. When the loop is securely on the left needle, allow the stitch on the right needle to drop off. Again, repeat this action until all your stitches have been worked onto your left needle. You have now purled a row of stitches. If you continue alternating a knit row with a purl row you have created the Stocking Stitch. The right or knit side is smooth, whereas, the

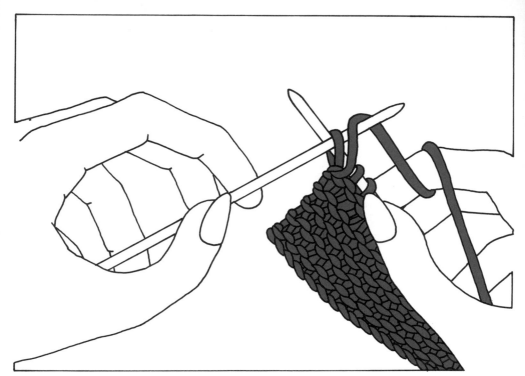

Two stages of the Purl Stitch

purl or reversed Stocking Stitch is ridged and looks similar to the Garter Stitch.

Garments made of the Stocking Stitch are the most popular pattern. However, they need edgings of either the Garter Stitch or combinations of knit and purl to keep them from curling up.

If you are knitting a fabric in the round on either four needles or the circular needle, the right side or Stocking Stitch side will always be facing you. Therefore, you achieve the smooth texture of the Stocking Stitch by knitting every row.

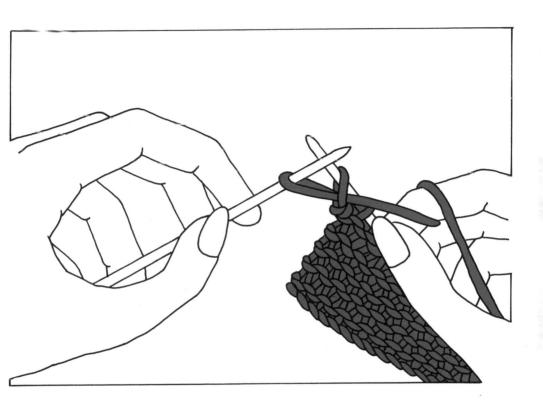

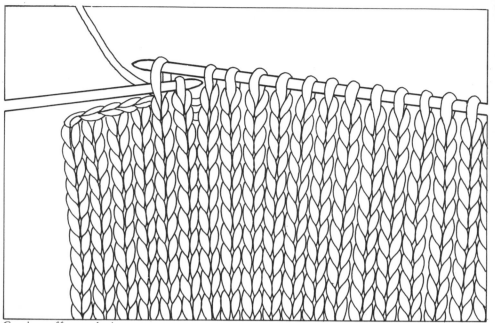

Casting off on a knit row

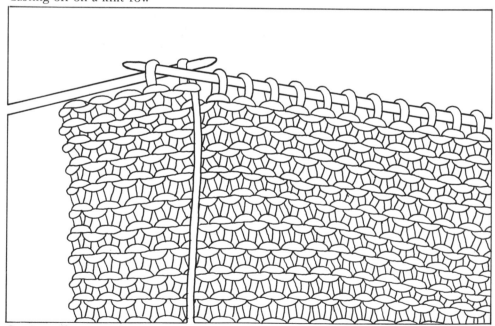

Casting off on a purl row

Casting Off

This is the method of creating a selvedge finish to a piece of knitting. The binding off, as it is sometimes called, is necessary to keep the fabric you have created from unraveling. Since it is important to keep this finishing work elastic and lying loosely, some knitters use a larger size needle for this particular part of the work. If you have bound off too tightly, the selvedge row may contract.

Knit the first two stitches on to your left needle. Using the tip of the right needle, lift the first stitch over the second and allow it to slip into the work. You are now left with one stitch on your left needle. Knit the next stitch from the right needle on to your left needle and repeat the lifting of the first stitch over the second and allow the stitch to drop off. Continue in this manner until there is one stitch remaining on your left needle. If the casting off is to complete a part of the garment, you now cut the yarn with about four inches (10 cm) to spare, draw it through the remaining stitch, and pull to tighten.

If you are casting off a set number of stitches to create shaping, just continue working as you have been directed in your pattern. The stitch on your left needle is counted as one of the remaining stitches.

If you are casting off on a purl row, purl each stitch and cast off in the same manner as for the knit stitch.

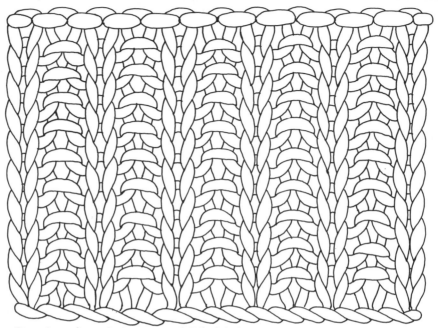

Drawing of one knit, one purl Rib Stitch

Drawing of three knit, one purl Rib Stitch

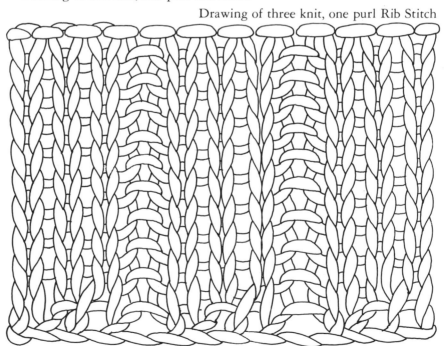

More Basic Stitches

A knitter can go along merrily for many years using the basic stitches, that is, the combination of the knit and purl stitches. The next series of stitches are just that.

The best way to become proficient in these is to knit a series of four-inch (10 cm) squares. You will then become aware of what the stitch pattern may require. They are based on a multiple of stitches which is necessary to complete the pattern.

Some stitch patterns require multiples, of two, three, four, or five stitches; some may require multiples plus a fixed number of stitches. For example, if the stitch requires multiples of three, plus two, you will have to cast on eleven, fourteen, seventeen stitches or however many are necessary to give the required width to knit the stitch.

Rib Stitch. This is one of the most useful of stitches. It is elastic, springs back into shape and is perfect for cuffs, some necklines, and hip-fitting ribbing on sweaters.

One and One Ribbing. Cast on an even number of stitches. Knit the first stitch, purl the second stitch, repeat until the end of the row. Your second row and all subsequent rows will be guided by having the knit stitches fall over a knit stitch in the previous row and the purl stitches fall over the previous purl stitch.

Ribbing can also be fabricated in rows of two knit, two purl, or, for a change of pace, three knit and one purl. These two variations require casting on in multiples of four.

The first row of the three knit and one purl ribbing should have a slight variation after casting on. Weave a single row of one knit, one purl. This will keep the predominant stocking stitch in the ribbing from curling up. Your second row will then begin with the three knit, one purl. All subsequent rows will have the stitches fall into line following this row.

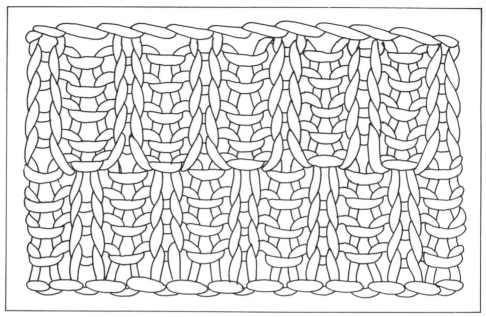

Drawing of one knit, one purl Broken Rib pattern

Broken Rib Patterns. This interesting variation of the rib pattern is simple to use for flat fabric such as baby carriage covers. It will not have as much elasticity as the straight ribbing, and therefore is not recommended for sweater cuffs or welting.

If you use the broken rib pattern, keep in mind that the proportions must increase as the rib grows wider, as you will see from the following instructions.

One and One Broken Rib. Cast on stitches in multiples of two.

1st row through 4th row inclusive K1, P1, repeat to the end.
5th row through 8th row inclusive P1, K1, repeat to the end.
Repeat these eight rows.

Three and Three Broken Rib. Cast on stitches in multiples of six.

1st to 8th row inclusive K3, P3, repeat to the end.
8th to 16th row inclusive P3, K3, repeat to the end.
Repeat these sixteen rows.

Notice how the number of rows must increase as the ribs become wider.

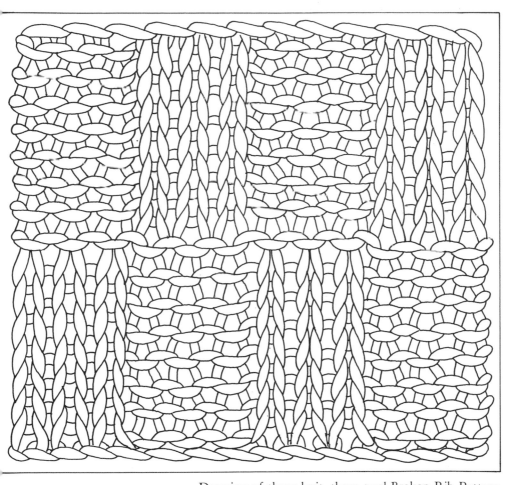

Drawing of three knit, three purl Broken Rib Pattern

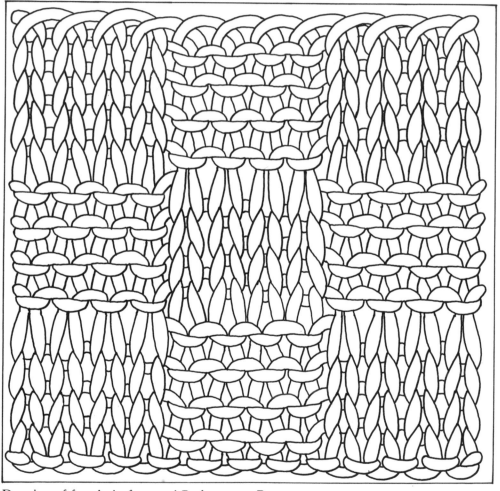

Drawing of four knit, four purl Basketweave Pattern

Basketweave Stitches. The two and two Basketweave Stitch is sometimes called the Double Moss Stitch. This pattern is strong and flat; again, like the Broken Rib Stitch, it does not have the elasticity needed for welting. It is often knitted in thick wool and is part of the traditional pattern found in Aran knitted garments. This small weave makes an attractive, warm cover for baby cribs or carriages.

Cast on stitches in multiples of four.

1st and 2nd row K2, P2. Repeat to the end.

3rd and 4th row P2, K2. Repeat to the end.

Repeat these four rows at least twice again and you will see the emerging pattern.

Four and four Basketweave Stitch is the large repeat of the two and two pattern. It makes a handsome, warm bedcover when heavy rug yarn is used.

Cast on stitches in multiples of eight.

1st to 4th row inclusive K4, P4. Repeat to the end.

5th to 8th row inclusive P4, K4. Repeat to the end.

Repeat these 8 rows.

Diamond or Brocade Stitch

The patterned placing of a knit or purl stitch can be used to create a design. Such is the Diamond Stitch, or Brocade Pattern, as it is sometimes called.

This pattern goes back in history—it was used in the undershirt worn by Charles I of England when he was executed. He is said to have asked for this particular garment because it would keep him warm. He did not want to shiver in the raw chill of the morning as it might be misinterpreted as fear.

The Diamond Pattern can be used in many types of yarn and is always fashionable.

Cast on stitches in multiples of six, plus one.

1st row K3 *p1 k5. Rep from * to last 4 sts p1 k3.

2nd row P2 *k1 p1 k1 p3. Rep from * to last 5 sts k1 p1 k1 p2.

3rd row *K1 p1 k3 p1. Rep from * to last st k1.

4th row *K1 p5. Rep from * to last st k1.

5th row As 3rd row.

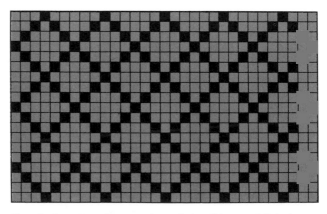

Graph showing the creation of the Diamond Stitch

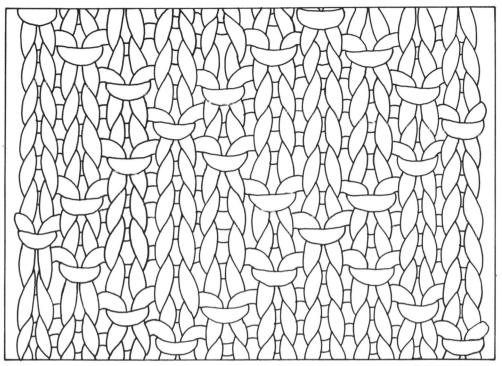

Drawing of the Diamond or Brocade Stitch

6th row As 2nd row.

Repeat these 6 rows.

You can create simple patterns of your own, such as including an initial or date in the knitting of a garment, to give it a distinctive personal touch.

Using the classic stocking stitch as background, make some practice samplers of your own. Begin by making a drawing on graph paper, each square to represent a stitch. Blacken the squares that are your design, number, or initial. These are your purl stitches. The white squares represent your knit stitches. Begin reading the graph as an instruction sheet. Read from the bottom left-hand corner. The rows on the right side are worked from left to right and are considered the odd-numbered rows. The wrong side or even-numbered rows are worked from right to left. Your right or stocking-stitch side will show the purl stitches as the design. The wrong side will show the design in knit stitches.

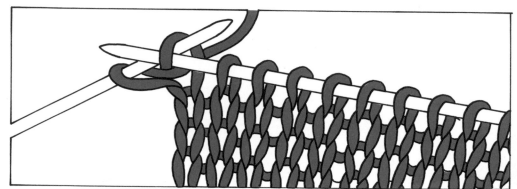

Increasing at the beginning of a row

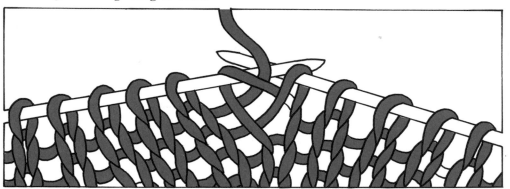

Increasing in the middle of a row ("invisible increasing")

Increasing and Decreasing

Increasing or decreasing in knitting requires combining the skill of creating your fabric and pattern both at the same time. It varies the number of stitches to either widen or narrow the fabric.

There are several methods of increasing. The first and simplest is increasing at the beginning and end of each row. To make a stitch at the beginning of a row, knit or purl the first stitch in the usual fashion, then knit or purl the second stitch but do not slip it off the right-hand needle. Instead, insert the point of the left-hand needle into the back yarn of the same stitch and knit or purl a stitch again. Then allow the stitch to slip off the right needle. If you are increasing at the end of a row, work until two stitches remain on the right-hand needle. Increase into the next-to-the-last stitch as you do at the beginning of the row, then work your last stitch in the usual manner. The creating of the increased stitches in this way will keep your edges neat.

If your pattern calls for increasing in the middle of a row, there are two simple methods. The first method—and the most certain to avoid an unsightly hole—is to insert your left-hand needle from front to back into the stitch in the row directly below the next stitch on the right-hand needle. Knit a stitch in the usual way, then continue to knit the stitches off the right-hand needle. If you are increasing on a purl row, have your yarn in front of the needles, bring the point of the left-hand needle through the stitch from back to front. Pick up the yarn and pull it through as for a purl stitch.

The second method can be a bit tricky. If it is not done properly, you may be left with a hole. Using the tip of the left needle, pick up the loop of yarn that lies between the stitch on your left-hand needle and right-hand needle. You must create a twist with this bit of yarn as you slip it on to your right-hand

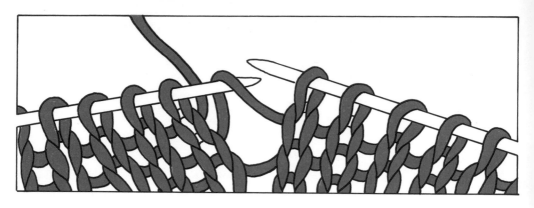

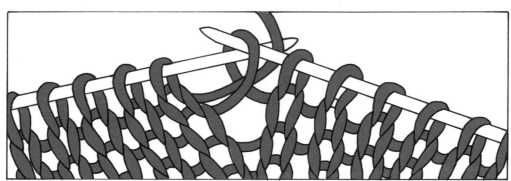

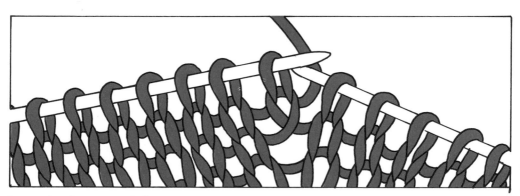

Increasing between stitches

needle, and then continue knitting in the usual manner. This method is not very satisfactory if you are increasing on a purl row. It is simpler and neater to use method number one.

Decreasing

The simplest way of decreasing is by working two stitches together. This may occur at the end of a row or at any point your pattern indicates.

To decrease on a knit row, simply knit two stitches together instead of the usual one. The top stitch will slant toward the right. The instructions will read "K2 tog." If you are decreasing on a purl row, purl two stitches together in the usual way. The top stitch will slant to the left. The instructions will read "P2 tog."

Decreasing by slipping a stitch is often used when "paired" increases are called for and the stitches must slope visibly in opposite directions.

For a decrease on the knit side of your fabric, slip the first stitch from the right needle to the left needle, then knit the next stitch. With the point of the right needle lift the slipped stitch over the knitted stitch and off the needle. The instructions will read "sl 1, K1, psso," and the top of this stitch will slant to the right.

If your decrease is on the purl row and is to be slanted to the left, your pattern will probably read "P2 tog tbl," that is, purl two together through the back loop. I have learned a simple stitch that will achieve the same results without having to maneuver the twist required for "P2 tog tbl." Read, practice and correct your pattern markings and you will sail through this stitch with ease.

Work up to the two stitches that are to be decreased. Purl the next stitch and *slip it back on to the right needle*. With the tip of the left needle, lift the stitch beyond over it and then *return the purled stitch to the left needle* since it has already been worked. You must always remember that the first stitch has to be returned to the left needle—don't make the mistake of working it again.

The major point to be kept in mind with any of these methods of decreasing is that when your fabric is facing you, what slants in one direction will appear in the reverse when you hold the fabric up against yourself.

Multiple decreasing is used for creating buttonholes or shaping a neckline. Work to the position in the row where your pattern indicates that decreasing is to take place. Knit the next two stitches and then cast off the required number of stitches in the usual manner. Note that the one stitch remaining on your left needle after casting off will be counted as part of the stitches still to be worked to the end of the row.

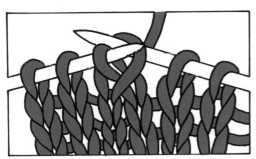 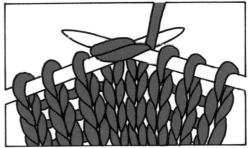

Drawing of decreasing method known as "slip one, knit one, pass slipped stitch over"

Decreasing on a knit row by knitting two together

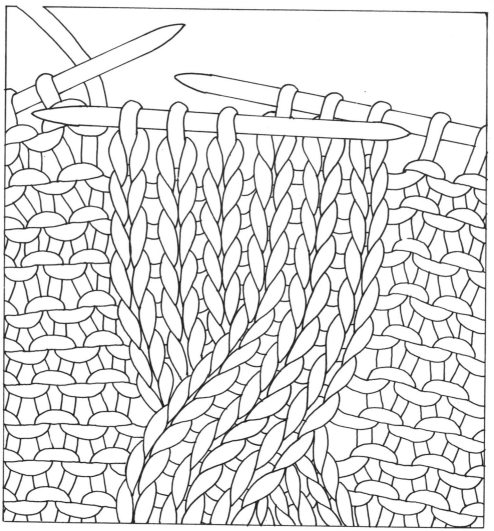

Drawing of cable twisting from left to right

Cable Stitch

This is a stitch with a long history. It originated in the fishing villages of Britain, and represents the rope life-lines of the fisherman at sea. Truly one of the simplest of the decorative stitches, the cable stitch gives depth and dimension to your knitting. It is usually worked against the background of purl stitches, and is based on the stitches being moved to another position in the same row. A short two-pointed needle, called a cable needle, is required. The variations on cable stitch have become more elaborate as time has gone by. Once you have mastered the basic cable, any variation will be simple to you.

The left-handed knitter must *reverse* the pattern instructions to achieve the effect of the cable going either to the left or to the right.

Careful work on a sample incorporating the instructions for cable twisting from left to right and then from right to left will

Cable stitches twisting from left to right
and then right to left

give you a clear picture of exactly how you can achieve your cable twist in the direction specified by your pattern.

Cast on 40 stitches.

1st row (Rs) P9, k6, p10, k6, p9.

2nd row K9, p6, k10, p6, k9.

3rd through 6th row inclusive Repeat the first two rows alternately.

7th row P9, slip the next 3 sts on to a cable needle and hold to the *front* of the work. With the left needle knit the next 3 sts from the right needle in the usual manner, then knit the 3 sts from the cable needle. This will twist your cable from the left to the right. Continue the row with p10, slip the next 3 sts on to the cable needle and hold to the *back* of the work. With the left needle knit the next 3 sts in the usual manner, then knit the 3 sts from the cable needle. This will twist your cable from right to left. Then P9 to complete the row.

8th row Repeat the 2nd row.

These 8 rows will give you a concise picture of the cable pattern.

Drawing of cable twisting from right to left

Trinity Stitch

A delightfully simple stitch that goes well with the cable stitches is a "bobble and twist" stitch with the formal name of the Trinity stitch. It is most frequently found in Aran sweaters. The right side of your knitting must be worked in purl stitch just as done for the cable stitch. The Trinity stitch can be placed between the columns of cable stitches. The name Trinity is derived from the methods of working three into one, and one into three.

For your practice cast on in multiples of 4 stitches.

1st row (Rs) P to the end.

2nd row *K1, p1, k1 all into the same stitch. P3 tog, repeat from * to the end.

3rd row P to the end.

4th row *P3 tog, k1, p1, k1 all into the same stitch. Repeat from * to the end.

Repeat these 4 rows at least once again and you will become aware of the small bump or "bobble" on the right or purl side. The wrong or knit side will show the "twist" that you have created.

Lobster Claw Stitch

Another stitch linked to the daily life of the fishermen that frequently appears in Aran knitting is this one depicting the cream of their fishing catch.

Cast on a number of stitches divisible by 9, plus 2—say, 38 stitches.

1st row P2, *k7, p2, repeat from * to the end.

2nd row K2, *p7, k2, repeat from * to the end.

3rd row P2, *slip 2 sts on to cable needle and hold at the back of the work, k1 from the right-hand needle, then k2 from the cable needle, k1, slip 1 st on to the cable needle and hold at the front of the work, k2 sts from the right needle then k1 from cable needle, p2 and repeat from * to the end.

4th row K2, *p7, k2, repeat from * to the end.

Repeat these 4 rows at least 5 times for a clear picture of the pattern.

Honeycomb Stitch

This variation of the cable stitch is smaller in size than the straight cable stitch. It too is part of the Aran tradition—it represents the beehives that the fishermen's wives tended while the men were away at sea.

Again, the left-handed knitter must reverse the pattern instructions so that the twisting and moving of the stitches will create the desired effect of the honeycomb.

If the pattern instructions read Cable 4 back, then you must Cable 4 front. When they read Cable 4 front, then change to Cable 4 back. Work the following sample for a clear picture of what you should knit.

Cast on a multiple of 8 stitches—32 stitches.

1st row *slip 2 sts on to the cable needle and hold at the front of the work; k2 sts from the right-hand needle, then k2 sts from the cable needle. Slip 2 sts on to the cable needle and hold it in back of the work; K2 sts from the right-hand needle then K2 from the cable needle. Repeat from * to the end of the row.

2nd row P to the end.
3rd row K to the end.
4th row P to the end.
5th row *C4b, c4f, repeat from * to the end of the row.
6th row P to the end.
7th row K to the end.
8th row P to the end.
Repeat these 8 rows at least 3 times.

Large Patterns

The next two patterns are larger in design than the stitches previously shown. You need from ten to twenty rows to give you a good view of the design.

These patterns also include instructions not previously given in other stitches, which can be put to many uses.

The lovely Pyramid Pattern includes two new instructions; the first is "K up 1." This simply means inserting the left needle from front to back, picking up a loop of yarn and drawing it through, leaving the stitch on the left needle. Pick-up knitting is frequently worked to finish neckbands or to add turtlenecks on sweaters. Your pattern will tell you exactly how many stitches are to be knitted up.

Sometimes it is necessary to knit up in the body of a garment. Hold the right side facing you, the yarn to be held on

Pyramid Stitch

the wrong side. Use a crochet hook inserted from front to back and draw the yarn through the stitches and slip onto your right needle. You are ready to begin following the pattern instructions with your left needle.

If your instructions read "P up 1," just pick up and purl. Hold your yarn in the purl position, bring your needle through from back to front and pick up a loop onto your left needle.

The second new instruction is noted as "Sl 1, k1, psso." Slip a stitch from your right needle on to your left without working the stitch. Knit the next stitch as usual, then with the tip of your right needle, lift the slipped stitch over your knitted stitch.

Cast on a number of stitches divisible by 15 plus 1—46 stitches.

1st row K to the end.

2nd row P4, *k8, p7, rep from * to last 12 stitches, k8, p4.

3rd row K1, *k up 1, k2, sl 1, k1, psso, p6, k2 tog, k2, k up 1, k1, rep from * to the end.

4th row P5, *k6, p9, rep from * to last 11 sts, k6, p5.

5th row K2, *k up 1, k2, sl 1, k1, psso, p4, k2 tog, k2, k up 1, k3, rep from * to last 14 sts, k up 1, k2, sl 1, k1, psso, p4, k2 tog, k2, k up 1, k2.

6th row, P6, *k4, p11, rep from * to last 10 sts, k4, p6.

7th row K3, *k up 1, k2, sl 1, k1, psso, p2, k2 tog, k2, k up 1,

Traveling Rib

k5, rep from * to last 13 sts, k up 1, k2, sl 1, k1, psso, p2, k2 tog, k2, k up 1, k3.

8th row P7, *k2, p13, rep from * to last 9 sts, k2, p7.

9th row K4, *k up 1, k2, sl 1, k1, psso, k2 tog, k2, k up 1, k7, rep from * to last 12 sts, k up 1, k2, sl 1, k1, psso, k2 tog, k2, k up 1, k4.

10th row P to the end.

These 10 rows will give you the pattern.

Traveling Rib is a simple way of moving a stitch without using the cable needle. The rib can be moved either to the left or right by knitting the stitch in the following manner.

To knit the rib twisting to the left, insert the left needle into the front of the second stitch on your right needle and knit, then knit the first stitch and slip both stitches off the needle together. This is sometimes abbreviated "K twl."

To knit the rib stitch twisting to the right, put the left needle behind the first stitch and knit into the back of the second stitch, then knit the first stitch and slip both off the needle together. This may be abbreviated "K twr."

Cast on a number of stitches divisible by 12, plus 2—14.

1st row P6, *k7, p5, rep from * to last 8 sts, k7, p1.

2nd row K1, *p7, k5, rep from * to last st, k1.

3rd row P5, *twl, k4, twl, p4, rep from * to last 9 sts, twl, k4, twl, p1.

4th row K2, *p7, k5, rep from * to end.

5th row P4, *twl, k4, twl, p4, rep from * to last 10 sts, twl, k4, twl, p2.

6th row K3, *p7, k5, rep from * to last 11 sts, p7, k4.

7th row P3, *twl, k4, twl, p4, rep from * to last 11 sts, twl, k4, twl, p3.

8th row K4, *p7, k5, rep from * to last 10 sts, p7, k3.

9th row P2, *twl, k4, twl, p4, rep from * to the end.

10th row K5, *p7, k5, rep from * to last 9 sts, p7, k2.

11th row P1, *twl, k4, twl, p4, rep from * to last st, p1.

12th row K6, *p7, k5, rep from * to last 8 sts, p7, k1.

13th row P1, *twr, k4, twr, p4, rep from * to last st, p1.

14th row Rep 10th row.

15th row P2, *twr, k4, twr, p4, rep from * to end.

16th row Rep 8th row.

17th row P3, *twr, k4, twr, p4, rep from * to last 11 sts, twr, k4, twr, p3.

18th row Rep 6th row.

19th row P4, *twr, k4, twr, p4, rep from * to last 10 sts, twr, k4, twr, p2.

20th row Rep 4th row.

21st row P4, *twr, k4, twr, p4, rep from * to last 9 sts, twr, k4, twr, p1.

22nd row Rep 2nd row.

Lace Knitting

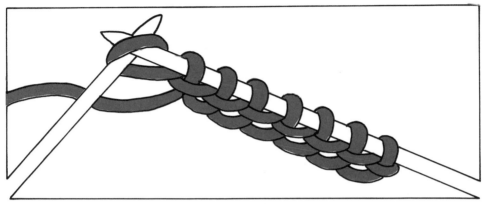

Casting on for lace knitting

Lace knitting is the most delicate of all knitting. The stitches are most effective if worked in cotton or a two-ply yarn, and the needles should be no larger than a number 3 (3.25 mm).

Avoid hard and thick edges in the casting on and casting off. Therefore, change your method of casting on. Cast on the first two stitches in the usual manner of the two-needle method. Then insert the left needle *into the second stitch*, draw a loop of yarn through, and transfer it to the right needle. Continue in this manner for the necessary number of stitches. When casting off, try to work loosely, using a needle a size or two larger.

Lace patterns are created by stitches made in a specific manner during the knitting of a row and often followed by knitting two or more stitches together.

The increase or making of a loop between knit stitches is made by bringing the yarn forward in front of your working

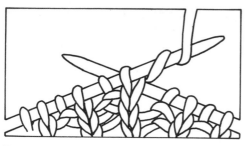

Lace increase between knit and purl.
Called "YRN"

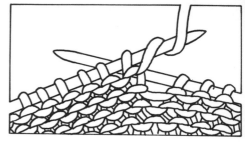

Lace increase between two purl stitches.
Called "YRN"

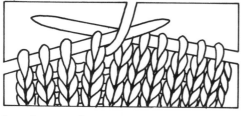

Lace increase between two knit stitches.
Called "YON"

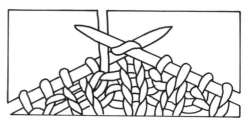

Lace increase between purl and knit
stitches. Called "YON"

or left needle. Wind it around the needle to bring it back into position for knitting the next stitch. This is sometimes abbreviated "yfwd," yarn forward, or "yon," yarn over needle. The newly created loop is not actually worked until the next row.

The increase between purl and knit stitch would again be marked "yon." Since the yarn is forward when the purl stitch is finished, it has to be taken over the needle to make a loop and have it correctly positioned for the knit stitch to follow.

If your increase comes between a knit stitch and a purl stitch it is called yarn round needle or "yrn." If the increase is worked between two purl stitches it is again "yrn" since it has to be wound around the needle to be brought back into position for the purl stitch.

The following stitches will give a good, general experience of lace knitting.

For Shale Stitch, cast on a number of stitches divisible by 11, plus 2—24.

1st row K to the end.

Shale Stitch

Faggoting Rib

2nd row P to the end.

3rd row K1, *k2 tog twice, yfwd, k3, yfwd 3 times, k2 tog twice, rep from * to last st, k1.

4th row P to the end.

Repeat these 4 rows at least once again for a clear view of the pattern.

For Faggoting Rib, cast on a number of stitches divisible by 5, plus 1—16.

1st row P1, *k2, yfwd, sl 1, k1, psso, p1, rep from * to the end.

2nd row K1, *p2, yrn, p2 tog, k1, rep from * to the end.

Repeat these rows several times for the pattern to emerge.

Dropped Stitches

Dropping a stitch can happen to any knitter. It is simple to rectify if you can catch it immediately, before it becomes a run, or ladder.

If you have dropped a knit stitch, insert the left needle through the loop from front to back and catch the missed strand. Pull it through and place on your left needle, then continue to knit. If your dropped stitch is on a purl row, insert the left needle through the back of the loop and catch the missed strand and transfer to your right needle and continue to purl.

If your dropped stitch becomes a run before you are aware of it, it can easily be rectified with a crochet hook. Hook each missed strand through the loop until you can place it securely on your needle. If you have finished and cast off that particular section of your work, use a tapestry needle threaded with your yarn and weave along the end catching the loop off the crochet hook as you reach it. Continue weaving the tapestry needle along until you are certain it is secure.

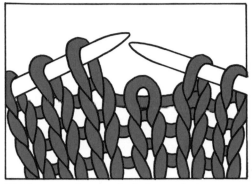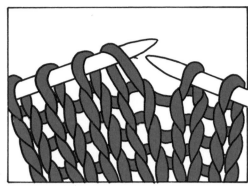

Picking up a dropped stitch on a knit row

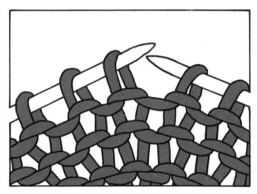

Picking up a dropped stitch on a purl row

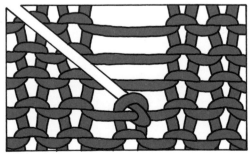

Using a crochet hook to pick up a run, or ladder, on a knit side

Using a crochet hook to pick up a run on a purl side

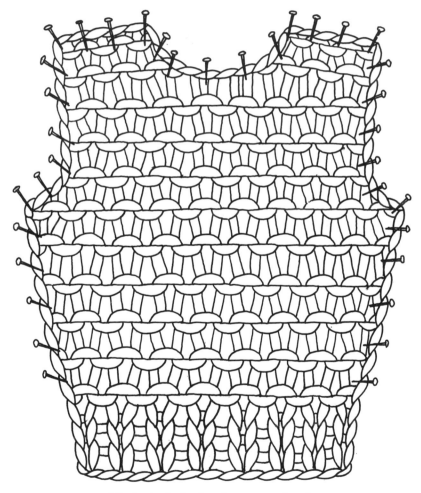

Method of pinning in preparation for
blocking and pressing

Blocking and Pressing

Many synthetic yarns used today may be ruined if they are pressed. The paper wrappers around your skeins or balls of yarn will usually give you cleaning, washing, and pressing instructions. Read carefully before blocking and pressing.

If blocking and pressing are recommended, proceed in the following manner.

Your standard ironing board may not be wide enough. Make an ironing pad using a folded blanket to create several soft thicknesses, and cover this with a sheet. Block each section separately, placing the knitted section right side down on the padding. Pin into place at the corners, making sure that you have not pulled the section out of shape, and take care that the stitches and rows are in a straight line. Now, using rustproof pins only, pin the sections into the padding about a half-inch (1¼ cm) apart. Using your rigid ruler, check all dimensions to be certain that they agree with the pattern size instructions.

Set the iron at the proper temperature for the fiber and place a clean cloth, either dampened or dry, over the knitting. Then press the iron down on the top of the cloth. *Do not move the iron back and forth*. Move to another part of the knitted fabric and repeat the action. Allow the knit fabric to cool and dry before removing the pins. Then go on to do the same with another section.

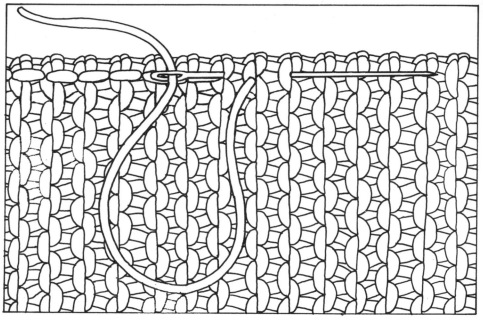

Back Stitch method of seaming

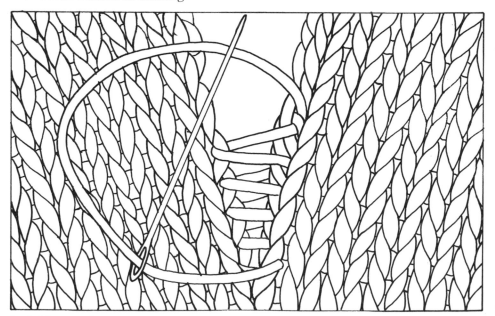

Invisible seaming

Seaming

Back Stitch Seaming. Hold the two sections to be seamed with the right sides together and work on the wrong side of the fabric. Using a tapestry needle with the knitting yarn, begin your seam working from left to right. Secure the yarn with two or three small stitches, one on top of the other; then bring your needle through to the back of the work. Move along to the right, bring the needle through to the front of the work the width of one knitted stitch from the end of the last stitch, and pull the yarn through. Take the needle back from the right to the left across the front and put it through to the back at the end of the last stitch. Bring the needle up again one stitch beyond the last stitch and continue until you have seamed the section.

Invisible Seaming. Place the two sections to be seamed on a flat surface with the right sides facing you, making certain that the sections are in proper alignment. Use a tapestry needle with your knitting yarn and secure the yarn at the lower edge of one of the sections. Pass the needle across to the other section and pick up one stitch, then pass the needle back to the first section and pick up one stitch. Continue working this way, pulling the stitches tightly so that they are invisible on the right side.

HAPPY WEARING!